The Snowman

In the skies above the trees so high,
A snowflake drifted from the sky.
It twirled and spun, so small and bright,
On a cold and quiet winter night.

The forest whispered soft and low,
As down, down, down, the flake did go.
Through branches bare, it floated free,
A tiny dancer full of glee.

It landed gently on the ground,
Joining others all around.
But this flake felt a magic glow,
And soon began to grow and grow.

It gathered friends both near and far,
Until it formed a shape bizarre.
A snowman tall with a big, round face,
Ready to dance all over the place.

He swayed and spun, his arms spread wide,
With joy and laughter, he couldn't hide.
The trees stood still in silent awe,
As the snowman danced without a flaw.

He leaped and twirled with joyful might,
His snowy form so pure and white.
With every spin, his smile grew bright,
As he danced beneath the moon's soft light.

The stars above began to fade,
As night prepared to make its trade.
But still, the snowman danced with grace,
In his snowy, secret place.

He danced with critters, big and small,
Who came to join the snowy ball.
The rabbits hopped with tiny feet,
Their joyful leaps were light and sweet.

The owls swooped down from trees so high,
Their wings outstretched against the sky.
They joined the dance in silent flight,
Gliding through the frosty night.

The foxes peeked from dens so deep,
Awake from their midwinter sleep.
They twirled and pranced with nimble grace,
Around the snowman's dancing space.

The bears, though slow, began to sway,
Awakened by the night's ballet.
With lumbering steps and heavy paws,
They joined the dance without a pause.

Then slowly came the morning light,
The snowman knew he'd danced all night.
He bowed his head, his dance complete,
As sunlight warmed him, soft and sweet.

As the sun began to rise,
A tear of joy fell from his eyes.
The night had passed in joyful play,
But now it was the start of day.

With one last twirl, he felt the glow,
As he became a flake of snow.
And up he rose into the sky,
Waving the forest a soft goodbye.

But who knows where the wind might blow,
Or where the next snowflake will go.
If the moon and temperature align just right,
Perhaps he'll dance in your town tonight.

Made in United States
Orlando, FL
10 December 2024

55357163R00018